BR**IT BALLOONS

> Five Years On

99 reasons in rhyme

By
Will B Justice

MAPLE
PUBLISHERS

BR**IT BALLOONS 99 reasons in rhyme

Author: Will B Justice

Copyright © 2026 Will B Justice

The right of Will B Justice to be identified as author of this work has been asserted by the author in accordance with section 77 and 78 of the Copyright, Designs and Patents Act 1988.

ISBN 978-1-83538-743-6 (Paperback)
978-1-83538-853-2 (Hardback)
978-1-83538-744-3 (E-Book)

Book Layout and Cover Design by:
White Magic Studios
www.whitemagicstudios.co.uk

Published by:
Maple Publishers
Fairbourne Drive, Atterbury,
Milton Keynes,
MK10 9RG, UK
www.maplepublishers.com

First edition published in October 2019 by
II Books Selkirk Scotland
Copyright (c) 2019 Ian Cheyne MA(Hons), BA(Hons), MBCS

A CIP catalogue record for this title is available from the British Library.

All rights reserved. No part of this book may be reproduced or translated by any form or by any means, electronic or mechanical, including photocopying, recording or by any information storage and retrieval system without written permission from the author.

The views expressed in this work are solely those of the author and do not reflect the opinions of Publishers, and the Publisher hereby disclaims any responsibility for them. This book should not be used as a substitute for the advice of a competent authority, admitted or authorized to advise on the subjects covered.

Dedication

This book is dedicated to my late father.
Sadly, I knew nothing of his aspirations,
and achievements in poetry and playwriting
until after his untimely death.
He would have been
99 in October 2019.

Acknowledgements

I acknowledge the fact that many sources have provided the incentives and the inspiration which have enabled this book to be created.

I admire the work of many poets from Auden to Zephania, not forgetting William Topaz McGonagall, somewhere in the middle.

Singled out for special mention, thanks, and, in some cases apologies, are the following:

Dylan Thomas, William Shakespeare, Robert Burns, Sylvia Plath, Stevie Smith, Walt Whitman, Spike Milligan, Edward Lear, Robert Frost, ee cummings, WB Yeats and, of course, WH Auden himself, whose work never fails to be of contemporary significance.

There are others to whom I would like to express my particular thanks.

Billy Connolly for his timeless humour and his unerring ability to find humour in all kinds of situations and circumstances, good and bad.

Stephen Fry, especially for his book, 'The Ode Less Travelled', thanks to which I have been able to alternate comfortably between the tragic and the comic—arguably a potentially life-saving skill.

And Boris Johnson who, again arguably, made it all possible.

And all three for the example of their dogged determination to carry on regardless. I have battled through my own problems myself. In all honesty I have now concluded that there is no longer any point in worrying—about anything!

Will B Justice
October 2019

Introduction

Will Justice was having a conversation one day, about recent parliamentary elections and the 2016 EU Referendum, with an acquaintance, who became quite passionate about the obligation to vote in such elections and related important decision-making opportunities. "...think of all the suffering involved in securing what became 'Universal Suffrage'...". WBJ agreed. But added that "...it should also be an obligation on all who vote to do so responsibly, and be properly informed before casting their vote..."

Not long afterwards, WBJ came across some comments which had been made by voters in the EU Referendum. At first he was sceptical but managed to find confirmation that these were in fact quite genuine statements.

Those comments quoted in this book were made by means of a variety of sources: internet blogs and forums, social media, radio and television phone-ins, and other publicly available sources.

The resulting poetry is an extrapolation/interpolation, of the original statements. A variety of narratives and narrative voices have emerged during the writing of the poems. Also a variety of poetry forms have been used—something like 15 different ones—in an effort to reflect the range and nature of the views expressed. There are examples of the well known *sonnet*, the *villanelle* and even the *limerick*. Others perhaps less familiar include the *nonet*, *triolet* and something called 'ramble 'n' rhyme'.

Each comment has been treated according to its own merits. Some are serious, with varying degrees of innuendo and subtlety. Others are just plain silly. And, of course, there are the quietly pensive... and, seemingly desperately sad.

Each poem, both in content and form, is intended to reflect the, at times, fractious, fragile, flippant and often uninformed nature of the expressed opinions—together with any *political incorrectness*, some of which is likely to be considered offensive.

It is hoped that the finished work in some way exemplifies, and just as importantly, amplifies some of the many reasons given for voting to either leave or remain within the European Union.

Ian Cheyne for II Books, Scotland

October 2019

(First published edition)

Introduction to January 2025 edition.

It is now five years since the withdrawal which 'Brexit' initiated was completed.

Five years on and there are issues constantly arising from the decision for the United Kingdom to leave the European Union.

For these, and many other reasons, the voters' comments which lead to the creation of this book are still valid within the context of the EU Referendum, and in a larger context of democracy in general.

For these reasons, along with the encouragement from many who acquired a copy of the original publication, it has been decided to re-publish the original, largely as it was with only one or two minor updates/corrections.

Ian Cheyne (for WB Justice)

January 2025, Scotland.

Bibliography

Fry, Stephen, *The Ode Less Travelled* United Kingdom: Hutchinson, 2005.

The Poems

70

Br**It Balloons

1

The whole thing is a mess,
I wish I could care less,
Please make it go away,
Saved for a rainy day;
It keeps me wide awake,
I need a healthy break,
Maybe the French won't mind,
The Germans show they're kind,
Leave Brussels to the sprouts
Now that there's lots of doubts;
Not cap in hand
Please understand,
We're not sure what to do;
Perhaps you're not sure too?

28

2

*I'm a pro at protesting
And proud of it;
Done it for years,
Have no fears, if you want someone to shout
Just look out for me,
I'm always here.*

*I would have remained
But as I've explained
I need to dissent,
Behaving like sheep doesn't help you to keep
Your identity, see?
I'm made different.*

"...to give Cameron a better negotiating position..."

73

3

Cameron always gets it right
Even when he gets it wrong,
I heard him give a speech one night
And he really was on song.

He said that we would quite soon have
A referendum for fun,
There was no need but just to prove
We're united one to one.

But rather than a stronger place
The leavers beat the remains,
Cameron left with rapid pace
And huge indelible stains.

Negotiations demand strength
Of purpose as well as mind,
Now all is dithering at length

On solutions we can't find.
Cameron can't negotiate,
He can't do better now he's gone,
So has it all been left too late?
Has too much damage been done?

90

4

They say that we all want to leave
But is that true, do they deceive?
They say that we have got a plan
But do they say that man to man?
They say we're better off outside,
But outside what, who will decide?
They say we're better off alone,
But who is it who's on their own?
They say we need to be together,
But is that England, or whatever?
They say that Scotland wants to stay
But where is that, and in which way?
They say what Northern Ireland needs,
But they're conjoined, so that impedes,
They say that Wales is in this too,
But is in what, there's no clear view,
They say a lot of things, it seems,
But are they schemes or just pipe dreams?
They say a lot, but who are they?
Well, no-one knows,
They didn't say!

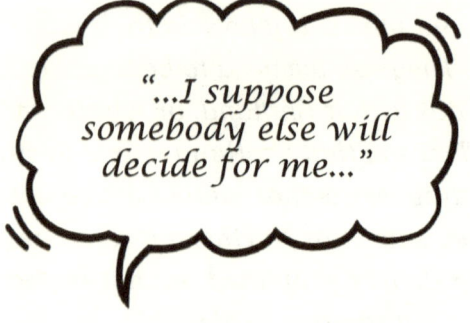

58

5

I didn't want to vote, really,
but thought I ought because I could
and nearly everybody says you should.
"Think of the suffragettes...and women
running in front of race horses...', of course
I never understood,
But it seems I should know
that the passionate show no mercy,
not even I daresay to themselves;
I've always felt compassion for anyone less
fortunate than me,
but it's not always easy to see them,
when you're imprisoned
in your own fears and miseries.
I think my get out of jail free
it seems is being able to see
not failing to know what it all means;
Yet I get stuck in this limbo
with nowhere to go.
Hoping some day someone else
will find a way to make up their mind,
and mine.
Meantime; a new norm.
Slouching towards complacency; to reform

87

Br**It Balloons

Isn't it exciting?
Isn't it all fun?
You'll just go on fighting
Long after it's all done,
Most folk say they want to stay,
I want it to be close,
So I'll will vote to leave today
And then I'll know I've had my say,
You know you wouldn't want it
Any other way,
Why so morose?

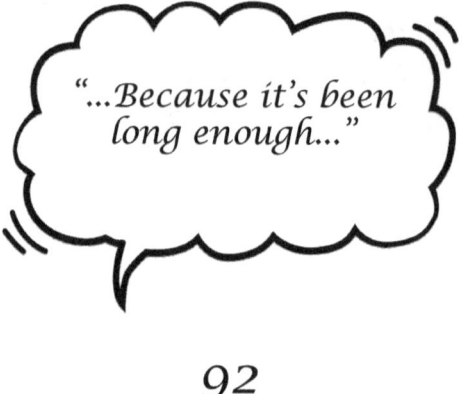

92

7

Nearly half a century, a lifetime,
maybe many of them,
New generations.
New hopes.
New highs.
New boredoms.
The wheel turns yet must be re-invented,
To deny is to die, unfulfilled.
Let's start running now.
No time to waste
Hasten
Back to the beginning
The grave is waiting
Hurry
Hurry
Don't wait.
But wait...
Too late.

11

8

I think it's time I got myself a life,
can't waste my days just sitting on the fence,
I voted leave just to annoy my wife.

So often now our arguments are rife
our disagreements growing more intense,
I think it's time I got myself a life.

Her wounding words cut through me like a knife
though I try hard, it seems to make no sense,
I voted leave just to annoy my wife.

And now I've voted there is no relief,
I feel like I've committed some offence,
I think it's time I got myself a life.

She stares at me as though I were a thief,
her gift of guilt gives me no recompense,
I voted leave just to annoy my wife.

I wonder now is there an afterlife?
A sanctuary where I need no defence,
I think it's time I got myself a life,
I voted leave just to annoy my wife.

18

Br**It Balloons

9

We must leave now, it must be understood,
We can't afford to wait another day,
Because Her Majesty said that we should.

There's been much anger in the neighbourhood,
Children crying that they would like to stay,
We must leave now, it must be understood.

We've thought about it hard and it's no good,
There is now doubt, we can no longer stay,
Because Her Majesty said that we should.

It hasn't worked out how we hoped it would,
The whole thing must be viewed with great dismay,
We must leave now, it must be understood.

The Common Market dream is gone for good,
We praise our Queen, we're happy to obey,
Because Her Majesty said that we should.

We find that we're no longer in the mood
To accommodate a court that hides away,
We must leave now, it must be understood,
Because Her Majesty said that we should.

17

10

*We send the mail to each and every one,
inform or frighten makes no difference,
for good and bad until the job is done.*

*We tick the box in shadow and in sun,
for us no sensitivity no sense,
we send the mail to each and every one.*

*We send regardless; battles may be won
behind closed doors, fear or fun, no pretence,
for good and bad until the job is done.*

*We play the game knowing that some would run
to burden others with weakness their defence,
we send the mail to each and every one.*

*We fire the bullets though we have no gun,
bearing no guilt we offer no defence,
for good and bad until the job is done.*

*No moral rules impede us once begun,
Life is difficult, there's no recompense,
we send the mail to each and everyone.
for good and bad until the job is done.*

70

11

There was a time in my old school day,
when just fifty million lived here,
ten million more have now come to stay,
one more Greater London, I fear.
England has suffered much more than the rest,
but that's no reason to scoff,
we need to cut numbers, and ensure that the rest
politely 'clear off'!

"...Because I felt uncomfortable with brown people on a bus the other day..."

22

12

Well you know; I don't like to say; but, well, really
do they have to stay?
You know I'm not black and white, like those old films;
I can be very colourful; oranges and greens, they're good
for you;
and reds and blues, very patriotic;
but browns; so depressing; so seventies; without the flare;
and look down; in fields and gardens; it's brown,
it's everywhere; and we don't need more;
we've got our share.

40

Br**It Balloons

13

An evil young sous chef from France,
When destroying left nothing to chance,
He could carbonize beef,
Scorch pork without grief,
And incinerate lamb at a glance.

32

14

They need little excuse to give Jews a bad name and it's always the same

old story; they all seem to rush to tar with the same brush, it's some kind of game

that's been played throughout history; so my friends say, and they know;

my neighbour votes labour and he thought that their saviour was Corbyn; not now;

my friends say he's anti-semitic and they're quite specific; they know: he should go;

just like the EU he denies that it's true but between me and you, my friends know;

the blokes down the pub, and those at the club, well, they read the right papers,

they know;

you don't have to go far to find facts in the 'Star' or the 'Sun' that will make up you're mind;

when all's said and done, they tell the truth, who's against Jews; just ask your friends,

or your tailor, it's easy to choose; right?; don't you know.

"...Because the EU has devoted 26,911 words to the regulation of cabbages..."

10

15

I've not been a lover of cabbages
they've not been a lover of me,
but I am prepared to defend them
for all people with whom they agree.
There's going to be new regulations
and the cabbage will suffer no doubt,
the EU's trying to constrain them,
next in line is the humble sprout.
So if kale and savoy are your flavour,
then join me against the EU.
Just think me a welcome saviour
of the poor humble cabbage, and you.

57

16

Can you walk along a street and not look back?
Can you walk alone and never fear attack?
I could do all these and never go off track,
The milk of human kindness I'd never lack,
To get on well with every face, I'd the knack,
But a growing hatred pins me to the rack,
The cards have been shuffled and I don't know the pack,
I turn each one in terror;
Knowing it may be black.

"...Because it takes more than 5 litres of water to flush my s**t away..."

99

17

As a child I learned to flush,
But not without a childish blush
To be reminded in front of others
Was often a reprimand of mother's,
Trying hard not to be upset,
Those distant fears I did forget;
That is until the present day;
Now EU laws have caused dismay;
More than 5 litres to wash my mess away?
What would mother say!

16

18

I'd never run a Marathon,
I've eaten quite a few,
But now the EU
Calls them Snickers;
My knickers!

Will B Justice

9

19

*Once, Faith was beamed upon benignly,
Adherents patronised by the assured atheist,
At worst, a figure of fun,
Battles between church bosses
Raged above their heads,
Ecumenically contrived in Cold War fashion,
Now the Islamic heat is on,
Overcooking our communities and culture,
Time for a cooling calming ex-communication.*

"...Sunderland's a giant Job Centre...voted to put everyone in the s**t like us..."

85

20

Living here is not amusing,
Sunderland, the name's confusing,
Is it South?
But we're up here and in the North
And unemployed, for what it's worth,
Tynemouth.

We must be generous and share
The s**t that lurks here everywhere,
The fun of signing on each day
Is freely ours to give away,
Have fun!

93

21

*It isn't clear who made this mess,
yet middle class and their betters must
admit their part much greater than the rest
of us, they who betrayed our trust.*

*They used to have a 'toffee-nose' stuck up,
unlike the others, nostrils held high skywards,
afraid of looking down upon themselves, to stop
the view of those bounders on the ground, blackguards.*

*What is that smell?
Who can tell?
The adhesion of blame
Reeks of Hell's Legions.*

"...Because fishermen now won't have to throw fish back..."

37

22

It always seems not to smack of common sense,
to throw fish back shows a lack of sensibility,
an offence to the fish
who expressed no wish
to be free from the sea;
so ask me; can I sense a better way of doing things?
Not sitting on the fence
I'll say, in my defence,
what could be worse
than not catching them first?

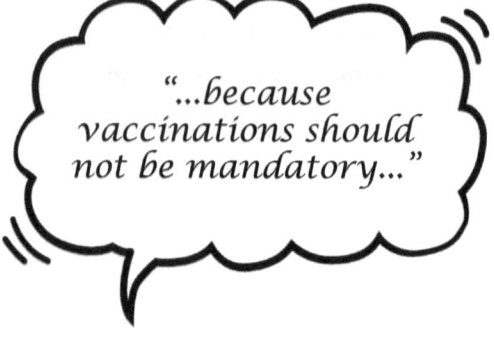

69

23

I never vaccillate over vaccinations,
I reject the current machinations,
Now that we have been forced as a nation
To accept the vaccine laws;
Never should we be enslaved
To this needless cause.

I protect my children's health all by myself,
Big business has robbed us of our medical wealth,
Corporate messes must be matched by personal stealth,
We'll make our own immunity,
EU out; UK in;
Our community.

"...send them women in headscarves back home...stole my mother's purse..."

25

Br**It Balloons

24

There used to be a day when it was so easy to say
what lurked beneath the headscarf,
the lumps and bumps, the happy humps of hairdo's
in the making, could always get a laugh from any half-baked humourist
of music hall and club Saturday nights,
it was our right.
Now we cannot know if these headscarves are for show,
or hiding places, signs of under-cover designs and cultural secrecy,
offendable sacred customs reign here?
We have paid dear
for our welcoming embrace of cash, clothing and arms
plucked from our own needy
and their conspicuous poverty.
Stolen wealth,
For unknown stealth.

98

25

What is TTIP? Some transatlantic mystery?
Shopping across a different sea it seems is a solution;
To what? To me it's just another place I'd rather not be;
And can we have acronym-free, please?
I know the BBC, and ITV, and both AA's,
And I cherish the days when home was best
And not invaded by http; and the rest;
My stall was set up and the Common Market was there for all to see
Across the Channel:
And it was simple,
My own desert island, close at hand.

63

26

No need to obey those EU laws,
They gave us no say in a single clause,
The important things have just been ignored,
Useless ideas will be put to the sword,
With a single stroke we will scythe away,
The bureaucrats waste will have had its day;
Too much foreign lingo has addled our brains,
Now we can stay here and greet the remains;
Our own laws are simple and fair to see,
From now on we'll all live in harmony,
Though should we find ourselves in a mess
Then at least it is ours, no need for redress,
Finally re-united as a single nation,
We then will enjoy our own consternation,
After a fashion,
Again.

47

27

I really fancied a change,
but couldn't quite rearrange
my thoughts beyond my dreams,
being practical it seems
is never easy;
though it keeps my mind busy
and free from unpleasantries
which would otherwise burden me
with desires to rule the world
or within the thresh-hold
of my home I might be king;
if it weren't for that thing;
that need to be constantly
inconstant and seeking
a change.
Perhaps I'll rearrange
Me.

46

28

Blocking	Choking	Puddling
Poking	Raging	Smoking
Heaving	Invoking	Puffing
Fuming	Working	Cursing
Floating	Bloating	Voting
Leaving	Believing	Relieving
Scaffolding	Guttering	Muttering

"...Because the EU parliament building is the same shape as the Tower of Babel..."

29

29

The EU wants a building
Just like the Tower of Babel,
They want it put up right away,
As soon as they are able.

The EU wants a building,
That symbolises evil,
It seems that we will have no say,
That's why there's this upheaval.

The EU wants a building
Far grander than the rest,
And once again it's just the same,
We'll come off second best.

The EU wants a building
Where language is confounded,
A useless shell, a shameless smell
Of emptiness unbounded.

59

30

Standing still in Sittingbourne,
Congealed by congestion;
Losing will in Sittingbourne,
Armchair occupation;
Motoring not moving;
Living life languidly;
Probably past improving?
New day of the week?
Nocarday?
Your day?
Never my day!

66

31

Bedroom taxation,
Both front and back vexation,
Breeding instant insomnia,
Bloody frustration.

65

32

China is the place where the Chinks were born,
China is the place where they should return,
China is the plate I eat off every day,
China is not my mate,
Please make it go away.

33

It seems there's very little we can do,
We may be back to forks before the fire,
Toasters will be banned by the EU.

It makes me wonder what else they might do,
What other mindless schemes may yet transpire,
It seems there's very little we can do.

One time we shared an optimistic view,
Our future hopes are now a funeral pyre,
Toasters will be banned by the EU.

Of simple joys we're left with very few,
New laws have daily dashed our hearts desire,
It seems there's very little we can do.

The time has come to fight, for me and you,
To raise our nation's banner on each spire,
Toasters will be banned by the EU.

Let's cling on to the values we hold true,
And raise our toasting forks ever higher,
It seems there's very little we can do,
Toasters will be banned by the EU.

"...Because if we stop all the immigrants using the NHS it will work again..."

19

34

*To get the NHS to work again
we must reduce demands that are upon it,
but are we now more ill or in greater pain?
I'm assured, just like my friends, that is not it.*

*The answer is there's more of us around;
when I say us the meaning is quite sound,
the NHS is treating more of them,
with fewer doctors worked into the ground,
it's immigration that the EU must stem.*

61

35

I hungered for a super-hoover,
Worrying all my waking thoughts,
Now sorrowful sleepless nights
Are destroying the dreams
Of swept starry stairs;
Dimmed dashed and crushed,
With my hopes,
Turned to
Dust.

36

More money spent. More
Money lent. More
Cash wanted. More
Joys junketed. More
Paintings bought. More
Fortunes wrought. More
Art today. More...
Get the picture?

37

Saturday night television was special before videos suspended animation;
As a nation we were best at the big occasion living for live spectacle,
Show-stopping songs and sunny sing-alongs.
They've spoilt it now;
Eurovision;
One time everything stopped for it; and tea;
The grandstand of the year,
Or was; it used to be;
Nobody votes for us no more;
And the attitude is ingratitude;
Fondness for other flavours now the UK's out of favour
Even though we've been their saviour, this churlish childish behaviour
Rankles every time;
There's no reason or rhyme;
So we'll leave them to climb back up again
On their own;
And they will moan
Just like our children
Leaving home to be
Alone;
Just like us,
Soon to be in
Splendid isolation.

49

38

I'm certainly not the violent type,
But I'd started to think the time was ripe,
I feared quite soon that I'd believe the hype
About why we're leaving,
The papers daily fed us with tripe,
The leavers were deceiving.

I stay a stalwart steadfast remainer,
To me the issues couldn't be plainer,
For Cameron it was a no-brainer,
But he forgot Scotland
And the Silver Darling as late campaigner
To defeat the "indy" band.

Lessons not learned, doomed before it began
The remain's campaign useless to a man,
Getting it wrong, Cameron soon ran,
I voted leave and so fulfilled my plan
To give him a bloody nose.

"...Because EU taxes are making our petrol more expensive than everywhere else..."

77

39

Scintillating and disintegrating downwardly diving
Aiming in turn and in time at the bottom
Of a deep blue sea, or whatever colour,
Blue or red, the sky overhead happened to be;
Dying creatures mulching and squelching clutching
Layer upon layer of black sludge'
...and the Esso sign says happy motoring...
Why do we still delve into oily shelves
Now it should be possible to leave them be?
The cost is ever mounting as we descend
Repeatedly into Earth's fragile crust
Exhuming and exhaling exhausted fumes
So that life-sucking taxes may be stoked
To fuel private greed and yet another and more
Public con; time for sun and wind to drive us home.
...keep going well, keep going Shell...
We can be scintillatingly integratingly rising
Arriving in turn and in time at the bottom
Of the deep blue sky, or whatever colour, red or blue,
Is the hue of our nuclear passion this priceless day;
Look back on greed, and fuel wants with needs,
Not money to burn on Earth's bonfire.
...and the Esso sign is blown to hell...along with Shell...

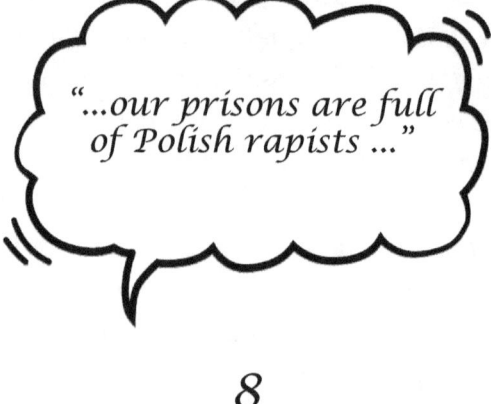

8

40

Prisons are full of Polish rapists,
And the EU allowed them in here,
Barely room for our villains,
Let alone Poland's worst;
So what can we do?
Just play the host
Or eject
Foreign
Beasts?

83

41

For some, fighting seems to be a pleasure
That they indulge in it at their leisure,
For others it's a mindless exercise;
Unlike peacefulness; a priceless treasure.

Regrettably it can never be wise
To simply ignore violent surprise,
When turning a cheek can lead to danger
To innocents, from those who terrorise.

I don't want my sons to harm or injure
At any time, never as challenger
With some unknown irregular army,
Standing with, and faced by, a stranger.

51

42

I admit that my home is archaic,
But I'm busy getting up to date
With a few of those photovoltaic
Panels, then my roof will look just great,
I did try to buy some quite recently,
Though my efforts met with little success,
I asked for a price, quite innocently,
To find I'd stirred up a real hornet's nest,
'There are panels which cost you a packet',
'The cheapest ones we can't give away',
It seems the whole business is a racket,
'However, China makes the best any day',
Now, the EU wants them to be dearer;
The need to vote leave couldn't be clearer.

91

43

Lavish lunches not lost on the EU,
Excessive expense-accounts day by day,
Where will it end?
Shortly, my friend;
Coffers were full,
Future's doubtful.

Insane indulgence breeds indigent strife,
Faceless figure-heads divorced from real life,
Their free healthcare
Leading nowhere;
False Viagra
Falls like Niagara.

"...Because a united Europe does not automatically result in peace..."

71

44

Perhaps unknowing, we possess a cornerstone
Of faith in Peace, a faith we sometimes take
For granted because it has become our own.

What was happiness is hastily outgrown
By us, and for us, shed with silent ache
Of each experience, as we live life alone.

A faded out feud which once was a gnawing bone
Of contention, a near fatal mistake,
Now half-forgotten, failed causes unknown.

Peace prospers, patently a concessionary loan
From depleted war chests, a chaste enforced break
From fighting, a seductively sweet tritone.

44

Br**It Balloons

45

*We can grow closer to Norway
And simplify our way of life
By reducing our daily wants
And the amount of land
We build houses on
To a fraction
Of today
Yes? No
Way*

69

46

Reflecting on our losing "desperanto',
Once more I will enjoy our Christmas panto,
The jargon without meaning
Featured first in our spring-cleaning,
The damage done we've set about to undo.

No longer stuck with "subsidiarity'
We can enjoy our language with new clarity,
There is "harmonisation'
Throughout our refreshed nation,
As we, once more, restore "singularity'.

Wonderful new ideas we are gleaning,
We see our true selves, never overweening,
And should we ever find the need
To once again be deceived,
Then our home-spun lies will be much less demeaning.

76

47

And what will you do with your money, my son?
What will you do, will you have lots of fun?
"I'll invite all my friends to come round for a party,
I'll fill up with booze and I'll laugh myself hearty,
I'll seek out the company of great glitterati,
I'll go back to school, be a new literati,
I'll give up the fags and I'll take up karate,"
It could be hard, will it be hard, it might be hard, it will be hard,
With just three hundred quid—to have a ball!

"... the EU will show a lot more interest in Britain's opinions when we're not in it..."

64

48

Noo that Britain's safe awa,
Far frae Brussels' constant pain,
No-one's heart will break in twa,
Should we ne'er go back again,
And as we boost our British Isles,
To the envy o' them a',
We can expect more EU wiles,
Set to steal our joys awa'.

Will ye no' come back again?
Will ye no'come back again?
Better lo'ed you'll ever be,
Will ye no'come back again?

49

49

Once branded as the biggest market ever,
Wringing out much debate and decades-long wait,
Trumpeted as transforming the common good,
Constantly cautioned, we shouldn't be too late,
Uttering ultimatums, now or never,
Reassuring mutterings, couldn't be bad.

Cold-war optimism swift to eschew bad,
Brightly eyeing the safest future ever,
Blackest days now distanced from our lives, never
To return, the chance is here to take, don't wait;
They lived a lifetime each day; mustn't be late
To form and strengthen friendships for the good.

War-time fears endlessly endured hoping that good
Would evermore eradicate the bad,
Permanent peace prevailing, not too late,
Finding a fresh freedom lasting for ever,
Welcomely wrenched from the agonising wait,
Long time coming, sometimes seemingly never.

Vaunted exclamations that there would never
Be anything gained through the EU but good,
Throughout the test of two world wars we've had to wait,
Hopeful soon to happily erase the bad
Blood between us and Germany, hopeful ever
Of real friendship, hopeful it's never too late.

Will B Justice

So much in common, seemingly strong of late,
Such similarities that there should never
Have been conflicts between us, we should ever
Be toiling together for our greater good,
Emptying out everything utterly bad,
Restoring, reassuring, so why the wait?

We find we are constantly constrained to wait
For Germany to get here, why are they late?,
Without their wisdom, what might have worked went bad,
Knowing their might was missing maybe we never
Would have spurned the comfort of "having it so good"
Membership proved our biggest mistake, ever!

Once glad, but now bad, did it ever work?,
Once good, but never truly justified,
Wanted to wait, you see; now it's too late.

Br**It Balloons

42

Br**It Balloons

50

When all's said and done it could be quite nice,
Though it may not seem very much to you,
To have the right to use my teabags twice.

To some it may appear to be a vice,
To enjoy a refreshingly lighter brew;
When all's said and done it could be quite nice.

It has been known to serve cold tea with ice,
So is it wrong to accommodate a few
To have the right to use their teabags twice?

I once tried tea which had been laced with spice,
Regrettably for me, a heady stew;
When all's said and done it could be quite nice.

Some like tea which has been brewed with rice,
If this is true, I stake my claim anew
To have the right to use my teabags twice.

To those who doubt may I give this advice?
Whatever we may choose this still rings true,
When all's said and done it could be quite nice
To have the right to use my teabags twice.

"...because giant wind turbines are no better than 'hamsterpower'..."

33

51

One time the 'Windmills of your Mind'
Was a pleasant popular song,
Windmills of a different kind
Now remind us that something's wrong,
'It isn't easy being green',
Another song describes our plight,
Wind gives power which can't be seen,
But no excuse for blatant blight,
Electricity can be had
By better means than gross turbines,
They're 'hamster-power', so it's mad
To strew our land with stone-age shrines,
It was an EU-inflicted crime,
We'll find a better way, in time.

"...Because you won't need to worry if you don't know your MEP..."

92

Br**It Balloons

52

*The time has come
it must be said
to talk of other things
like whether there
is better weather
or comfier bed-springs
or
how we'll spend
to no real end
an MEP's earnings*

*the time has gone
to live in fear
of ignorance
of things
of never knowing
MEP's names
and secret
meanderings
or why
we voted
and for who we
did without
knowing
anything*

12

54

Oh, the EU is like a dead, dead rose,
That never came to bloom;
Oh, the EU is like a melody
That can't be played in tune.

As now thou art a bonnie mess
So deeply sad am I;
And there will be a mess, my dear,
'Till a' the seas gang dry:

'Till a' the seas gang dry, my dear,
And earth boils with the sun;
I still can see the mess, my dear,
It's there 'till Kingdom come.

And fare the weel, our one time hope,
And fare the weel, a while!
And who knows will you come again,
Tho' it be ten thousand mile?

55

Br**It Balloons

55

*Beautiful Common Market of our yesterday
With your tariff free borders built in a wonderful way
Along with all your special arrangements in grand array
Which people know will stand for many a day
And we know we will enjoy them without dismay
So that this wond'rous thing makes many of us say
We need to look around no more
Nor cast our eyes to a distant foreign shore
For none is more beautiful to be seen
From John O' Groats to bonnie Paddington Green.*

*Oh Beautiful Common Market of our yesterday
Which has been constructed well by Mr Heath and Co, they say,
And we know that they will be proud for many a day
To see the glorious things they have put our way
So that we need have no fear nor dismay
That this wonderful thing will fade away
And we all can be happily sure
That the Common Market will last for ever more
And will be beautiful to be seen
From Scotland's big cities to the bonnie Bethnal Green.*

*Oh, Beautiful Common Market of our yesterday
Built as though you had great steel girders to help you stay
Just like the famous railway bridge of the silvery Tay
Everyone who sees you will exclaim that you cannot rust away*

Will B Justice

And that you will be joyous to behold for many a day
Making sure that people who have lots of things to sell you will not dismay
That they will be able to make all the money they need what's more
And not have to keep travelling to some foreign shore
But can instead enjoy the bonnie Magdalen which is a beautiful green
As well as all the parks owned by Her Majesty the Queen.

Br**It Balloons

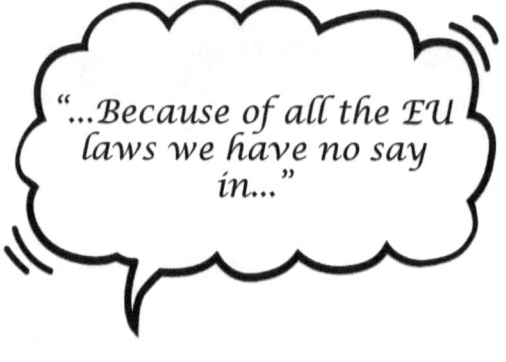

26

56

They make up new laws every day,
Laws in which we don't have any say,
I ask you just what kind of way
Is that to run things?
It's just another kind of way
To play at fun things.

It seems to be some sort of game,
One that's played with rules we cannot name,
Looks like it will remain the same
Our future is black
So long as there's someone to blame
If we can't fight back.

26

57

Fed up. Nobody listening. Downcast. Something missing.
They don't care.
They're everywhere
But here, where they're needed.
What's the point? I'll wreck the joint,
Or smoke it.
Not joking,
Just poking fun at misery.

95

58

Those mindless masters put us right off track,
I voted to join and now I rue the day
So now it's time to get our lightbulbs back.

Before the Common Market did we lack
The initiative and skills to pay our way?
Those mindless masters put us right off track.

We stood alone and fought off the attack,
And winning through we saw the light of day,
So now it's time to get our lightbulbs back.

We had the nerve to fight when things were black,
And we helped some others find their way,
Those mindless masters put us right off track.

We gave no rights for others to ransack
Our culture, or our loyalty betray,
So now it's time to get our lightbulbs back.

Decades ago they should have got the sack,
Bureaucracies all benefits outweigh,
Those mindless masters put us right off track,
So now it's time to get our lightbulbs back.

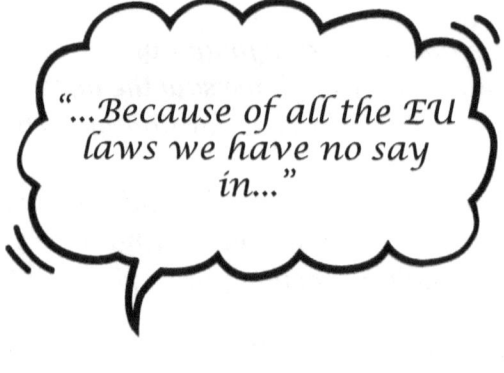

82

59

Of EU laws this much is true
They were not made by me and you;
They each day bring increasing pain,
They each day show how little gain
There is for us to stay, we few.

As we go on we ache anew
As lies from politicians spew;
We view them with endured disdain,
We view them through the crazy pane
Of EU laws.

As we their fiscal efforts view,
Our knuckles white, air turning blue,
We climb aboard the Eurotrain
Bound for Blighty and its sane
Conspicuous deceit, not wooed
By EU laws.

58

60

Muslim women can't wear make-up, I'm told,
Unless their husbands say that it's okay,
I vowed that I'd decide when I grew old,
I'm very glad that things turned out my way,
And if this Muslim wife allows her master
To tell her what she can, and cannot do,
She will not feel the thrill of having plaster
Fill out the occasional crack or two,
Or joys of blacking lashes for a party
And licking lips in deep seduction red,
She'll never know the fun of laughing hearty
On finding she's still wearing it in bed,
Now is that face made up, or is it pale?,
It's very hard to tell beneath a veil.

22

61

We conjure up the truth to fit the facts,
We tell the tales that others want to hear,
We know the Wiki secrets and their acts,
We populate the phantom world with fear.

We tell the tales that others want to hear,
Although they do not always think it so,
We populate the phantom world with fear,
Though seeds of angry winds may start to grow.

Although they do not always think it so,
We can persuade them ever to be fooled,
Though seeds of angry winds may start to grow,
By stealth and innuendo they are ruled.

We can persuade them always to be fooled,
We know the Wiki secrets and their acts,
By stealth and innuendo they are ruled,
We conjure up the truth to fit the facts.

78

62

They closed down all our mines,
That's why our wealth declines,
No wond'ring whether
Must dig together,
For treasured times.

They shut down all our pits,
Our business fell to bits
But we will win through,
All we have to do
Is use our wits.

An empire lost by stealth
To dubious commonwealth,
No good in pining
For silver lining,
Seek golden health.

We're on our own again,
We've ditched the gravy train,
The euro-scroungers
And towel-draped loungers
We may disdain.

Let's reinstate our miners
And build once more big liners,
Upon known devils
We'll risk our revels,
No decliners.

40

Br**It Balloons

63

Who cares about Greece?
They lost their marbles,
When I was a child I lost mine,
I cried for a while,
But I regained my smile
When I stole someone else's, in time.

They want to send cash
To be spent in a flash
On ouzo or some kind of wine,
We need the money
To buy ourselves honey,
To make up for lack of sunshine.

The old Greeks were wise,
They played with marbles
Although they were made out of stone,
It was always a game
Regardless of name,
They should play it again,
And not moan.

"...Because I want Britain to be the way it was in the 50's..."

77

64

The golden days of bright depression and shiny expensive newness; warming up to a cold war

And walls of brand new homes and nations; telly was black and white and cars were coloured;

And giant Wagon Wheels; Saturday nights of family fun around the box, no sex or violence

On a fourteen inch screen of decaying greys and games and crooning minstrels crooked

Through vertiginous vertical holds gone wrong, their songs reflecting harmonies of creed and race;

The pace was changed but different in a time of post-rationing plenty at popular prices

Which could never be afforded but had to be had; and it wasn't all bad, but sad;

Not yet time to forget; ever simple it seems but not ever easy; pained;

And it never rained.

99

Br**It Balloons

65

Each day we hand over lots of money,
Each day we pay out much more than the rest,
Each day we find this business isn't funny,
Each day they rob our children's treasure chest,
Each day we ask ourselves the same old question,
Each day we know the answer's just the same,
Each day we see that someone's failed to mention
Each day they have to play the same old game,
Each day our Government evades the issue,
Each day they turn a deaf ear to our cries,
Each day they blow our noses and say "bless you',
Each day they fail to ever wonder why,
Each day they don't know why they're on the rack,
We don't like giving and not getting back.

"*...Because there are too many Pakistan people in Glasgow...*"

24

66

We used to call Pakis Pakis
And nobody seemed to mind,
We used to call Paddy's Paddy's
Never knowingly unkind,
One time we would laugh at ourselves,
But that seems so long ago,
Our sense of humour is lacking
Now that Pakistan's come to Glasgow.

4

67

Africa is not in Europe, not on my map,
There's that middle sea which splits them up;
Why is the EU there?
Why should I really care?
Is it trying to join them?
So that we all play the same game?

Is this the start of an invasion, another war?
It seems to me that this time they have gone too far;
The EU is not an empire
And yet they seem to conspire
To conquer like Napoleon,
What happens if someone takes them on?

I don't know what the EU is doing down there,
But it's long past time to shape our future here;
We had a Common Market
Something many would like to forget,
Come back, it's too bloody hot,
Too late now though, to stop the rot.

> "...Because now our lads will get out of prison, cos there will be jobs for them..."

78

Br**It Balloons

68

Not his fault, really,
We always tried our best,
Born into poverty.

They didn't help him,
Arrested him in his prime,
Forced into prison life.

Led astray he was,
Not enough to go round,
Just crafted into crime.

Jobs are coming soon,
Life opportunity,
Sons shoehorned into work.

Don't you see what you've done?
Stolen their years from them,
Look forward to hard labour.

98

Br**It Balloons

69

*At times it may matter more or less
How bureaucrats are come by, who picks them,
Or are they plucked out of a deep top hat
Which is bottomless?*

*At times it would be better to chatter less
And ask more; to know in what way there is a say
In these decisions, than make debate
Which is pointless.*

*Every vote must carry the same weight,
Yet there is no elation in election
Behind closed doors, as they do the Pope,
Which is hopeless.*

5

Br**It Balloons

70

*Felt it was time we should
Get things straight,
Once in a while there are
Ditherings;
May not seem much to you,
Honestly;
I've found that I can be
Hesitant;
So why unbend bananas when it's us who spend our money?
As consumers it's not funny to be confronted
With a straight fruit
Which does not meet our deepest needs;
It's unnerving and undeserving, when it isn't curving.*

"...because I couldn't decide... and my boyfriend voted to remain..."

29

71

Never able to make a decision
I'd dallied with the idea of remain,
The only other option was to leave,
Oh had there been a third way to bring joy?
Thoughts of never having had it so good
Would not have made my situation bad.

I wondered would it really be so bad
If I made a slightly wrong decision?
Others might consider my choice was good;
Those who thought it better to remain
Would be filled with unbridled joy
Just like the majority voting leave.

I could have been persuaded to go for leave,
Consoling myself that it mightn't be too bad
Though I may not have felt the deepest joy,
No-one could deride me for my decision,
And after, I might possibly remain
The one who ultimately did good.

The question we should ask is what is good?
And whether this would be the case with leave?
Perhaps a safer bet would be remain
Which many voters thought might not be bad,
One way right or one way wrong, a decision
Fraught with prospects of very little joy.

Will B Justice

Someone's misery can be another's joy,
Unacceptable can often turn out good,
The agonising part, the decision,
Is the thing that we'd all prefer to leave
To others who have no fear of looking bad,
Who are happy for their mark to remain.

The happiness in voting for remain
Perhaps may lead to everlasting joy,
Blind optimism blanking out the bad,
Rose-tinted views where everything is good,
That is except for those who voted leave,
Whose blunt choice became the best decision.

We made our choice not knowing good or bad,
A post-Eden puzzle, a decision of little joy,
To bereave with leave or stain with remain.

Br**It Balloons

12

Br**It Balloons

72

I read all Enid Blyton as a child,
She satisfied my young imagination,
The thought of summers camping in the wild
Rescued me from studying stagnation,
Her children were a different class from me,
Endless days of sunshine I seemed to miss,
Never five, but often we could make three,
And trios of fun could sometimes be bliss;
Wild exploits never took us far from home,
We had to stick to straw caves in a field,
Unlike the "famous five' we didn't roam
To magic lands like venturers of old;
Now at last the adventure has begun,
Leaving the EU might actually be fun.

Will B Justice

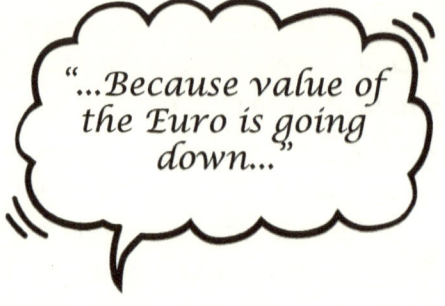

95

73

The value of the euro is falling,
The pound may be the safest bet,
Put in a sterling effort,
Soon to exude success,
Britain rich again,
Need no handouts,
Sufficient
Unto
Us.

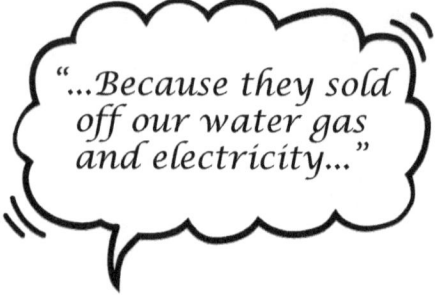

71

74

They sold the lot,
Our water, you see,
Sold our gas
And electricity.

It's time we knew
If there's any more
They'll take from us,
We must be sure.

Time and again
We've been fed with lies,
The EU's greed
Was our demise.

Utilities
Were our monopoly,
One time was strong,
Our stability.

They won't return,
So we want them out,
Let's all depart
Those years of drought.

53

75

School Nativities, a seasonal joy,
Enactments of the Perfect Gift,
Expressions of hopes and fears
Threatened by another god
With a different name,
Message the same,
To Islam
On Earth
Peace.

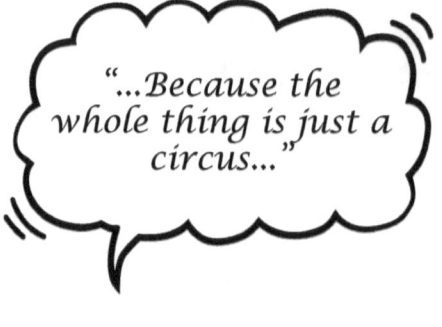

81

Br**It Balloons

76

Nobody heard us, the common man,
But still we were moaning;
Things were much worse than you thought;
And not governing but clowning.

Poor we, we'd always loved larking
But now we're dead.
The effort must have been too great, our hearts pounding
They said.
Oh, no no no, it was useless always,
Still we dead lay moaning;
They were too far out all our lives,
And not governing but clowning.

77

77

My relatives can often be divisive,
But we don't fight battles every day,
I've an uncle who's painfully indecisive,
Sometimes I feel like kicking him.
Each and every one of us has our say,
Though concluding comments may be derisive,
It seems that it is just our family's way,
But hearing the remain, or leave, directive,
My uncle's indecision arrived to stay,
Thoughts ever swayed by his sister's invective,
Now his future is decided for him.

51

78

I want to buy my sweets in ounces,
They want me to buy them in grammes,
I want to buy my sweets in ounces,
I did both systems in my exams,
I want to buy my sweets in ounces,
They want me to buy them in grammes,
I'm imperial and wised up to their scams.

"...Because they're building houses for Filipinos and it's blocking my view..."

14

Br**It Balloons

79

My friend visited Indonesia,
She said it was a beautiful country,
I tend to suffer from travel amnesia,
Can hardly recall my last shopping spree;
But now and again a name seems to stick,
The most recent has been the Philippines,
And the mention of it makes me feel sick,
Not only the name but just what it now means,
They're building new flats soon to block my view,
To house immigrants from those far islands,
Sadly my anger is starting to brew
At the thought of them stealing from my lands,
Don't know Filipinos so I can't fuss,
Unless, of course, they're imposed upon us.

"*...Because I wanted to see the look on their faces...when they lost...*"

85

Br**It Balloons

80

What is that joyous view in my sight?
Why has it taken so long?
Watching them wriggle fills me with delight,
I feel I could burst into song.

Whence is that vision which tested the trite?
How is complacency shaken,
Each of them filled with indelible fright
Now the decision's been taken.

What now for Blair who forced us to fight?
What now for Clarke's condescension?
Their expressions were etched in my mem'ry that night,
Now; democracy has their attention.

"... the ensuing recession is going to bring house prices down, and I can't afford one.."

24

Br**It Balloons

81

I've always wanted to buy my own house,
I've always wanted a home of our own,
I've not forgotten I promised my spouse
We'd get something good, but not a millstone,
Yet since the EU, house prices have soared,
Just keeping my word was becoming a dream,
Then something I read just struck the right chord
And voting to leave could further my scheme,
Departure would spark a huge recession,
Demand would reduce and house prices would fall,
I could fulfil a lifetime's obsession
And buy for us a baronial hall,
Vote leave, just like me, and have no concern,
We'll be doing both of us, a good turn.

"...Because leaving means we can pause immigration...choose new neighbours..."

2

Br**It Balloons

82

*As I gaze calmly through my window at night,
The street is all quiet and lit by the light
From neighbouring windows,
In this place where each knows
Each other's neighbour, and not just by sight.*

*Out there in the darkness there's nothing to fear,
No unknown and unwelcome terrors lurk here,
Now we've left the EU
There is nothing to do
But simply breath in the friendly atmosphere.*

*Since we're in charge we can make up our own mind,
And sometime in the future if we should find
The need for more leisure,
Then we, at our pleasure,
Can open our doors to the immigrant kind.*

"*...Because there will be no more insulting cities of culture...*"

68

83

There once was a 'city of culture',
Its name was Old-Big-Little-Thorpe,
On the map it looks like a vulture,
And exists in an endless time-warp.
The townsfolk were ever so grateful
For their fine cultural accolade,
But now they're suing the EU
For all the failed promises made,
The name of this town to the locals
Was one of great simplicity,
Now this has been publicly ruined
For the townsfolk of poor Oblitee,
So they are exceedingly grateful
To be leaving the EU today,
At last they can renew their slumbers
And shoo poncy tourists away.

91

84

Henry Kissinger asked the question
What is the number I should call?
How to get London, England
Who to ring first of all?
Not just anybody
But one who knows
Me closely
One who
Shows
The others
The right way
To get things done
Just how they should run
The business which they claim
Is the fundamental reason
For their being in the game at all:
Or is it all simply just another gameshow?

"*...Because we will free to use 60 watt and 100 watt lightbulbs again...*"

1

85

Free to be bathed in extravagant light,
Leaving the EU dispatches the night,
All we can see now are friendly faces,
No-one is lurking, there's no more dark spaces.

Proudly our nation, illuminated,
Loudly our passions once understated
May brighten our minds and lighten our steps,
Rescuing us from those Stygian depths.

But new-found freedom can often be hard,
It's very important to remain on guard,
Ready to take a little meander,
Briefly, within the shades of Wallander.

37

Br**It Balloons

86

The sonnet has a well-balanced phrase,
As blank verse uttered in a single swathe,
Shakespeare favourite to condemn, and praise,
Its metre treading a well-trodden path,
But metres for me have sinned as Macbeth,
Murdered the measure borne by me at birth,
Bestowed on me with my first breath,
Walked with me as my feet stepped on earth,
Often have I inched my way to freedom,
I've celebrated with a yard of ale,
Imperial rule measures my kingdom,
Making the metre metallically pale;
Good enough to serve a million lifetimes,
And not the chilling blight of milligrammes.

"...Because before the EU that street over there used to be filled with shops..."

58

Br**It Balloons

87

I remember my mother used to shop
Without needing to leave our neighbourhood
And grandmother used our local co-op,
Their happy ways the test of time withstood,
Yet having battled through two great world wars
The cultural destruction was achieved
With the enactment of some alien laws,
Before we had the chance to be relieved,
Enburdened we became by foreign will,
Our sovereignty was now the highest stake,
I know within my heart we'd have them still,
Our neighbourhood fell, the price of our mistake,
One time that street out there was filled with shops,
Now it's become the place where no-one stops.

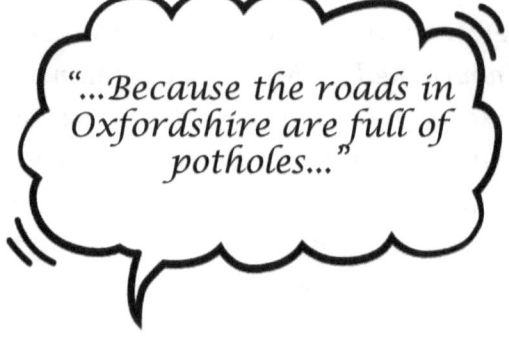

89

Br**It Balloons

88

The Beatles counted holes in Blackburn Lancashire,
Something like four thousand holes they found,
Now we've got four million more in Oxfordshire,
And there's more around.

Our roads are filled with holes now thanks to Brussels,
That's quite an inheritance we've gained,
To fill them in will exercise our muscles,
Would we had remained?

So now we have to search for many more holes,
Though some will find us first there is no doubt,
And when we're asked to fill in someone's straw poles,
Then fill them in with nowt.

95

89

It gets more unfair each and every day,
Prescriptions should be free for everyone,
It's only us in England who have to pay.

It's wrong that we didn't have any say,
That here they failed to speak to anyone,
It gets more unfair each and every day.

Who decided, just who says yeah or nay?
Decisions made before the job's begun,
It's only us in England who have to pay.

Scotland gets treated in a special way,
More money spent on each and every one,
It gets more unfair each and every day.

For all I know in Wales there's no delay,
Handing out all the cash until it's done,
It's only us in England who have to pay,

Do they expect us all to kneel and pray?
Or must we threaten with a loaded gun?
It gets more unfair each and every day,
It's only us in England who have to pay.

"...because I don't understand politics... that is what my friends suggested..."

25

90

It was never given to me
To understand, to help me see
The underhand skills and thrills
Of political jousting,
The rhetorical pasting
Of opponents,
The word that kills.

I rely on advice from friends
To keep me off the path that wends
Its way to depths of despair,
To rescue me from formless fears,
Restoring now the hope that cheers;
When I'm dead, will I really care?

I'm told that I should use my vote,
But knowing truth is so remote,
Voting badly can't be right,
Faith is simply assured hope,
Hoping the best, extending the rope
By which Parliament hangs, recondite.

63

91

What secret schemes cannot be seen behind the blatant veil
Which daily confronts our kindnesses?
The challenge is mischievous in its taunting intent,
Open faces and open minds greeted by bare-faced concealment;
Honesty need not hide behind false or foreign fashion
Casting doubts and outcasting its cultural unknowns,
Stolen from us is our trust and our truthful
Desires to value but not vindicate
First impressions;
Fetching or forbidding, we must always fail to find truths
Which are hidden.

"*...Because at least somebody here will have voted for our laws...*"

70

Br**It Balloons

92

United Kingdom Home Rule,
Contradiction in terms?
Sounds a little old school,
Like Celtic Nation berms.

Law and policy orphans
Will seem a little strange,
Home-grown pacts and paeans
We'll joyously arrange.

There's no fools like old fools,
Now happy with new chirms,
EU legal cesspools,
No longer cause for squirms.

Time for warring nations
To willingly exchange
Ideas for integration,
Productive counterchange.

Rescued from the whirlpool
Of unelected worms,
Be joyful and dry out
In Btu's and therms!

"...Because at least somebody here will have voted for our laws..."

28

93

Experts don't always get it right,
I'm assuming their leave predictions are all wrong,
Experts don't always get it right,
Economic gloom; fright not foresight,
Experts don't always get it right,
Safe assuming their leave predictions are all wrong,
Experts don't always get it right,
Safe assuming; why worry!; everything is wrong.

"...Because Brexit will magically resolve any problems in the British Economy ..."

73

94

It may be rather hard to see,
Just how an English Lit degree
Can give one a better insight
Into economic woes,
To plough productive furrows
In barren acres,
Putting our economy right.

Yet Michael Gove is on his game,
His novel skills may make his name,
Prosperity may yet depend
On such unlikely sources,
When unseen talent forces
Its way into our company,
To become a new-found friend.

Believing in magic potions
Though, may quite soon lead to notions
That waving a wand will cure
All our economy's ills,
Removing the need for skills
In running Britain:
Qualifications rich; jobs poor.

"...Wasn't sure but I want Boris as PM "cos he says wacky things, like him in the US..."

90

95

A funny chap in the States supports leave,
He's keen for us to quit without delay,
So does Boris have some tricks up his sleeve?

From dithering I can see no reprieve,
Does the US expect to save the day?
A funny chap in the States supports leave.

The EU strives constantly to deceive,
They claim that there is nothing left to say,
So does Boris have some tricks up his sleeve?

Retaining our humour isn't naive,
Saying wacky things is never child's play,
A funny chap in the States supports leave.

Our new PM I'm hopeful will achieve
Great things, if we just let him get his way,
So does Boris have some tricks up his sleeve?

Prophets of doom have forced us all to weave
Hopeful humour into our Misery Play,
A funny chap in the States supports leave,
So does Boris have some tricks up his sleeve?

> "...be able to rip off music..like China and Russia do...without those pesky EU controls..."

58

Br**It Balloons

96

(to the tune of "Frankie and Johnny')

*Ripping off music is okay,
Because I've been ripped off before,
Who needs a justification?,
To rip off a million or more...
It is my plan,
And I "aint doin' no wrong.*

*Music has been imitated,
For countless centuries,
It really is compliment'ry,
From Soviets to the swinging Chinese,
So that's my plan,
And I don't think it's wrong.*

*I've never abused law and order,
I know I'm a good citizen,
So why should the EU deny me
The same kind of kickbacks as them?
It was their plan,
And they sure got it wrong.*

*I relish all of those freedoms,
Which once again will be mine,
When I enjoy a great singer,
I like to spread the sunshine,
Yes, that's my plan,
And it just can't be wrong.*

"*...I don't mind my taxes supporting our own scroungers...*"

87

97

There's our poor and there's their poor,
And we can't take the blame for both,
It's clear from their demeanour,
That they'll lead us up that path;
There's our rich and there's their rich,
And it's always been that way,
Britain's taken for a soft touch,
Just another EU ploy;
There's our laws and there's their laws,
Which you think would be the same,
There's their highs and there's our lows,
Now it's time to fulfil the dream;

Charity begins at home,
And only time will tell
Whether every cloud has a silver lining?
And all's well that ends well.

"...bathed again in the glorious light of sovereignty..."

92

Br**It Balloons

98

As the glare of the cold day glints on me,
I wonder is this what I should expect?
Ferocious fighting had forced me to see
The dawn of a new nation, proudly erect.;
As I try to gaze through the gaudy haze
On this morning, this first day of freedom,
I see little, except for the sun's rays,
No sign yet of any brand new kingdom;
Instead more cries of independence needs,
From disenchanted thrawn celtic nations,
Barren soils have re-germinated seeds,
Disappointments re-ignited passions.
Was sovereignty ever a hope too vague?
Has stranglehold given way to plague?

> "...Because at least we'll still have Shakespeare..."

11

Br**It Balloons

99

Shall I compare thee to a summer's day?
My fervour now seems wild intemperate,
What were't that shook the darling buds of May?
The honeymoon was all too short of date.
Sometimes too soon the hope of heaven shines,
So often are its unseen workings dimmed;
And every time the hopeful search declines,
By chance, was absolute power untrimmed?
But should the cause of true worries not fade
Nor by halves but full promises thou ow'st;
Nor shall death not secure thee in his shade,
When by infernal means thou seek to grow'st,
So long as people have the eyes to see,
So then dies hope that breathed its life in thee.

Will B Justice

The Last Word?

(deliberately left blank)

Br**It Balloons

100

In our democratic dependency
The fundamental rules are always clear,
Respecting other's needs impeccably,
Absolute agreement is ever here,
Frantic fiction, mad misinformation
Seemingly seduced us into this place,
Still-born oaths, aborted machinations
Have turned us from the truths we have to face;
Mankind's aspirations, restless as the sea
Seek up-waves, with tangent tunnel vision,
Thoughtless of the troughs and their treachery,
Threatened ever by falsehood's derision;
The last view, lost in lies, unseeable,
The last word unspoken dies, unspeakable.

www.ingramcontent.com/pod-product-compliance
Lightning Source LLC
Chambersburg PA
CBHW020409080526
44584CB00014B/1249